P9-EER-922

MEDITATION

Linda Williamson

Bath · New York · Singapore · Hong Kong · Cologne · Delhi · Melbourne

This edition published by Parragon in 2007

Parragon
Queen Street House
4 Queen Street
Bath BA1 1HE, UK

Copyright © Parragon Books Ltd 2001

All rights reserved. No part of this publication may be
reproduced, stored in a retrieval system, or transmitted
in any form or by any means, electronic, mechanical,
photocopying, recording or otherwise, without the
prior written permission of the copyright owner.

Created by
THE BRIDGEWATER BOOK COMPANY

Cover Design by Parragon

A CIP catalogue record for this book is
available from the British Library

ISBN 978-1-4054-9740-4

Printed in China

contents

what is meditation?

Meditation means many things to many people. For some it is simply a way of relaxing. Others use it to bring about peace of mind. Spiritual seekers see it as a vital tool for connecting to deeper levels of reality.

Meditation has been used in the East for thousands of years, where it forms a central part of spiritual practice and discipline. The western world has been slower to appreciate its benefits. However, meditation is now becoming accepted not merely as a weird New Age pastime, but as a practical aid to inner growth and positive personal development.

Contrary to popular belief, meditation is not a passive activity. It is not a matter of closing your eyes and going into a trance or drifting off into a daydream. Rather, it is a means of actively focusing the mind on a single point of concentration. When this focus is achieved, something wonderful happens. The outer

BRAIN GAME **Students of meditation have to learn how to soothe the "monkey mind" that clutters our attention with thoughts and worries.**

mind, the "monkey mind" as Buddhists call it, which is always darting restlessly from one thought to another, slows down. The meditator enters a state in which he or she is totally centered, and mind, body, and spirit are brought into harmony.

Meditation is a transforming process that can ultimately reach into every aspect of our lives. It is the first step in a magical journey of self-discovery.

SPIRITUAL KEY *The practice of meditation has been used in religions such as Buddhism throughout history to attain spiritual enlightenment.*

INNER WORLD *When we start to explore our inner selves we are embarking on an amazing journey—on which life-changing discoveries are made.*

5

benefits of meditation

Meditation brings benefits on all levels of our being. Physically, it has been shown to lower blood pressure, strengthen the immune system, banish insomnia, and aid pain control.

Total well-being

Emotionally, meditation calms us down. It helps us to rise above all the conflicting emotions, hopes, desires, anxieties, and fears that shape and sometimes distort our thinking. Through regular practice, we

learn how to enter a still space in the mind in which all these feelings are seen as transient and ultimately unimportant in the scheme of things. From this perspective, we discover what really matters, where we are in life, and where we are going.

This inner tranquillity brings with it greater clarity of mind. We cope better with stress and can work more effectively. We become more tolerant and loving in our relationships with others.

But the most significant benefit of meditation is in our spiritual development. Many people today are looking for something to believe in. They sense that there is a spiritual dimension to life, but

REAL REWARDS *In the stress and busyness of today's world, it is easy to start feeling out of control. Meditation can help us to keep a proper perspective on life and to be able to cope with difficult everyday experiences.*

they are dissatisfied with traditional religions and dogmas. Meditation leads us inward, to our deep center, where we touch the eternal spirit within. Here, we find our own truth and discover an infinite source of wisdom and love.

STILL WATERS *Just as the sun reflects clearly off still waters, so the world is seen most clearly by a serene mind. Stress distorts reality and makes things seem much worse than they are.*

NO MYSTERY *Meditation is a journey—so the sooner you start, the sooner you start enjoying its many rewards.*

7

getting started

Everyone can learn to meditate. All it takes is patience and perseverance. You don't have to be religious or into "far-out philosophies." Before you start, you need to create the right conditions.

Meditation space

Ideally, you should set aside a room which is kept only for meditation, where the spiritual energy you generate can build up and be held. If, like most people, you cannot afford the luxury of a meditation room, choose somewhere—perhaps a corner of your bedroom—where you can sit and meditate without being disturbed.

This area should be simply furnished. All you need is an upright chair (not an armchair) and a table. Keep the room neat and tidy. Open the window frequently to

BASIC SETUP *The physical requirements for meditation are few. Use a straight-backed chair, not an armchair.*

let in fresh air to cleanse it. Decorate it with pictures you find uplifting and keep fresh flowers there. This is your special place, your sanctuary.

Try to make time to meditate every day. You don't need long: 10 or 15 minutes is enough to start with, increasing to half an hour or more as you become more experienced. Quality is definitely better than quantity! Early morning is generally considered the best time for meditation, while your mind is still fresh and before you become absorbed in the business of the day. If you cannot manage this, the next best time is the evening. But the most important thing is to choose the time that suits you and stick to it. Good, regular practice acts to condition and train the mind. You'll find that the more regularly and often you practice, the easier meditation becomes.

FLOWER POWER *Fresh flowers are a soothing refreshing presence in any room. Use them in your sacred space to keep your mind engaged and focused.*

posture

The traditional posture for meditation in the East is the lotus posture. However, it can be hard to maintain this position. Meditation does not go well with cramp!

Sitting comfortably?

Fortunately, you can meditate just as well sitting on a chair, as long as it is firm and upright. Take care before you start that your spine is erect. Your whole body should be comfortable: poised but relaxed, your feet firmly on the floor, hands resting lightly on your knees or in your lap.

You do not need to wear any special clothing. Once again, the first rule is comfort: don't wear anything too tight. The idea is to forget about the body so that the mind can be free.

Make sure that the room is suitably lit: dim and restful, but not too dark. The temperature should be pleasantly warm, but not overly

SEMI LOTUS *If you can't quite manage the lotus position, try sitting cross-legged on the floor. If you don't have carpet or rugs down, sit on a thin pillow.*

hot. All these preparations will help you to adopt the correct mental attitude—and make it less likely that you will fall asleep.

When you first start to meditate, it can be hard to ignore outside noise. You will be in a highly sensitive state in which loud noises or interruptions jar the nerves. So make the family promise not to disturb you, disconnect the telephone, then shut the door. You are now ready to begin your adventure of self-discovery.

BACK STRAIGHT *If you use a chair for meditation, choose one with a straight back and spend a few moments before you meditate getting your spine upright.*

11

first steps

In order to meditate effectively you need to be relaxed. Most people carry far more tension than they realize, both in the body and in the mind. Until this is released, it is hard to enter into a condition of stillness.

Progressive relaxation exercise

 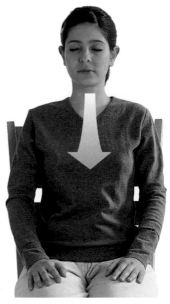

1 *Close your eyes. Make sure your spine is erect. Take a few deep breaths, drawing the breath deep down into your chest, feeling it expand. Just focus entirely on your breathing, allow other thoughts simply to come and then go.*

2 *Now expand your ribcage, then your upper chest. Hold the breath for a few seconds, then let it out gradually in reverse order, first from your upper chest, then the ribcage, and finally from your abdomen. Again, keep focused on your breathing.*

Step one

The relaxation procedure is very simple— but most meditation students find that it takes a few weeks of practice to get it right. You might need to go through it several times before you feel it has really worked. Don't hurry over this. Even if all you learn in your first few sessions is how to achieve a fully relaxed state, you will have learned a valuable lesson.

3 *Exhale until all the air is expelled. Hold the outbreath for a few seconds, then breathe in as before. Do this until you establish a comfortable, steady rhythm. Focus on your breath as it touches your lips and then reaches deep into your chest.*

4 *Now bring your attention to your feet. Tense the muscles of your toes, then relax them. As you do so, mentally command your toes to relax. Do the same with your feet and legs. Work your way up, tensing and releasing all the muscles in turn.*

relaxing your mind

Take another deep breath and, as you let it out, feel that you are breathing out all tension and anxiety so that you become freer and lighter. Enjoy these moments, when you can heal and nurture yourself.

INNER LESSONS *Focusing on your breath can help to bring insights about the essential flux of all things, from the tides of the oceans to the seasons and the natural cycles of life and death.*

More breath work

It is often thought that, in order to meditate, you have to make your mind go blank. This is almost impossible to achieve and, in fact, it is not necessary to try. It is far easier and more effective to give your mind something on which to focus. There are numerous techniques for doing this, some of which will be described later in the book. A very good exercise to start with involves the use of the breath.

BREATHING MEDITATION

Mindfulness of breathing, as breathing meditation is sometimes known, is one of the oldest, simplest, and perhaps most effective forms of meditation. It is meditation in its most essential form. It guides us toward giving our minds totally to the act of listening. Not to the sounds around us, but to the underlying meaning behind all existence. In this open state, the meditator is receptive to enlightenment.

14

Using the breath to still the mind

1 *Close your eyes and do the progressive relaxation exercise described on pages 12–13. Then let the breath fall into its natural rhythm.*

2 *Do not attempt to control it: merely observe. Be conscious of the air entering and leaving your nostrils. Note the rise and fall of your ribcage.*

3 *Focus on nothing but the breath. When other thoughts intrude, dismiss them gently without haste and return your attention to the breath.*

4 *After a while you will notice that something strange happens. You have the sensation that, rather than breathing, you are "being breathed."*

overcoming mental resistance

The exercise on page 15 might sound very simple, but in fact it is very difficult to perform. You will find that, as soon as you try to concentrate, all kinds of thoughts and images flood into your mind.

Interference

Bodily sensations become magnified. Your nose itches or you want to fidget. Outside noises seem unnaturally loud and startling. You might start drifting off to sleep, or else become bored and think you are wasting your time. Often it is the hands that want to fidget first—craving something to do.

Don't be discouraged by any of this. Everyone experiences these difficulties in the early days of meditation. The rational mind, which is used to being firmly in

WORLD RESIDUE *All of us have pressures and worries about our everyday lives that can interfere with meditation. Meditation helps make these worries less troubling.*

control of your thought processes, rebels when you set it aside and turn your attention inward. It behaves like a child that feels neglected and clamors for attention and entertainment.

So you can overcome the problem by treating it like a child. Be gentle, but firm. Refuse to give into its demands. Acknowledge the thoughts and sensations that inevitably arise, but do not allow yourself to be drawn into them. Simply view them as if from a distance, then refocus your attention.

It may be necessary to practice this technique time and time again, and there may well be occasions when you feel it is a hopeless task. But persevere—it will become easier with practice.

AMAZING BRAIN

The brain is an incredible organ, capable of thousands of calculations every second. In essence, we write a book every day with our constant thinking, worrying, and planning. Meditation puts us in touch with an equally amazing ability of our minds—one far more rewarding than intelligence or wit. With it we can get in touch with a spiritual level far beyond the experience of most people.

STRANGE NEW WORLD **When we start to meditate, our inner world can seem unfamiliar territory. With regular practice we become comfortable with ourselves.**

finding the point
of stillness

The key to successful meditation lies in performing a delicate balancing act. Your body must be held still, but without tension. You have to be relaxed, but not sleepy. Your mind needs to be receptive, but alert.

Central station

You might wonder how you can do all these apparently contradictory things at once. In time it will happen of its own accord if you just hold your mind fixed steady on one point of concentration.

This can be your breath. It can be an object, a word, a picture, such as an icon, or an idea. Whatever it is, the point of concentration is like an anchor in a stormy sea. For a long while the waves—the restless thoughts—surge around you and threaten to carry you away. But if you can hold onto the anchor long enough, the waves subside and the sea is calm. When this happens you experience a subtle, but

CALM IN THE STORM *As you persevere, the elusive moments of total peace will become easier to reach. This peace will impact on the rest of your life.*

important shift to an altered state of consciousness. There are no more interfering thoughts, just a gentle peace and an all-encompassing tranquillity.

You will have arrived at the still center, sometimes symbolized as a dot within a circle. This is the place where you become at one with your inner being.

SACRED SPACE
Meditation takes us to the sacred place within us. This is the place where mystics journeyed to commune with spiritual powers.

SEA OF TROUBLES *The way to the center of our being is strewn with turbulence. It takes perseverance to endure the storm.*

19

aids to meditation

There are many aids you can use to make your meditation easier and more enjoyable. While these cannot do the work for you, they can help to create the right atmosphere for calm, focused meditation.

Sacred smells

Incense has been valued for thousands of years for religious and spiritual ritual, cleansing, and bringing about altered states of consciousness. You can buy incense or joss sticks from any New Age shop, as well as many mainstream outlets. Incense also comes in small cones.

Ambient aromas

Aromatherapy oils, too, are an excellent aid. Frankincense, jasmine, and sandalwood are particularly suitable, either individually or in combination, but you can make up your own blends and experiment.

Heavenly sounds

Good music, playing softly in the background is relaxing. There are many New Age CDs and tapes designed specifically for use as

ATMOSPHERE *Oils, incense sticks, and flower essences can all be used to create a perfectly relaxing and yet stimulating atmosphere for meditation.*

meditation aids. Some people find that classical music, especially Mozart, raises the mind to a more spiritual level.

Subconscious way

Subliminal tapes work by bypassing the conscious level of mind which often acts as a barrier to deeper mental levels. They are programed with instructions which are too quiet for the conscious mind to hear, but which are received and acted upon by the subconscious. Subliminal video tapes are particularly powerful because they combine spoken suggestions with visual images.

Flowers on the brain

Flower essences are increasingly being used by meditators. In addition to the popular Bach flower remedies, there are numerous other adequate ranges now available. These operate on a subtle level, increasing spiritual awareness.

HELPING HANDS *Meditation aids can help you to focus, but they are not a replacement for simple will power and persistence. You still have to do the work.*

problem solving

Meditation will not make your life plain sailing or remove all your problems, but it will help you to deal with them. Meditation can help us to gain perspective and to make good decisions.

Practical spirituality

Through meditation, you become more sensitive and more able to empathize with others in their troubles. This gives you a better understanding of how they think and feel, enabling you to be less judgmental and more tolerant.

When you have a problem, begin your meditation session by stating the difficulty clearly to yourself. It may help to get things clear in your mind if you write them down. Then go into your meditation in the usual way. However, it is very important that you do not focus on the problem while you are meditating, it will only become more firmly embedded in your mind. Simply go within, seeking to find that still point of balance.

As you do this, insights may arise spontaneously. Suddenly you might see a way out of the difficulty or realize how you can handle the situation better. Even if this doesn't happen while you are actually meditating, don't be disappointed. Often

GOOD RELATIONS *Meditation helps us to become more understanding of other people. We can then use this knowledge in a loving and beneficial way.*

the answer will drop into your mind a day or two later, when you are relaxed and not thinking of anything in particular. It might also come in a dream.

Meditation helps you to connect with your own source of wisdom and inner intuition, which contains all the answers you need to cope with life's challenges.

INNER RESOURCES *Problems and worries always benefit from meditation. Write the problem down if this helps to clarify it for you. Meditate as normal, without focusing on the problem. Even if you don't get an answer, meditation will help you put the problem in perspective.*

23

creativity

Children are naturally creative. They play, dance, sing, and paint with no inhibitions, for the sheer joy of expressing themselves. Creativity is an essential part of human behavior that we shouldn't dismiss.

Art class

As we grow up, we learn to suppress this natural spontaneity. We dismiss our imagination as childish fantasy.

Meditation puts you in touch once more with your inner child and renews your sense of the joy and wonder of life. Many writers, artists, musicians, and people engaged in creative pursuits find inspiration through this means. It enables them to tap into a spring that constantly flows with fresh thoughts and ideas.

Try exploring your creative potential by having a supply of paper and coloring pencils on your table when you meditate. After a period of stillness, allow yourself to

CREATIVE KIT *Just a few pencils and scraps of paper are enough to help you express your creativity. Many of us grow up believing that we are not creative—in fact all of us have a creative aspect.*

draw or color. Don't worry about whether you have any artistic skill. Just go with the flow, letting your imagination be free and fully expressive.

Once you learn to link with your inner child in this way, you will find that you become more creative in all areas of your life. Gardening, cooking, writing a letter to a friend, or writing a report become opportunities for self-expression. You might surprise yourself with your hidden talents.

LOOSE REINS **When you start to express your creativity, just let your mind be free to follow whatever path it chooses. Don't worry about making sense—you're just exercising your creative muscles.**

mindfulness

In eastern monasteries, the monks and nuns spend much of their time carrying out menial tasks like raking the paths. How do they meditate then? In fact, any activity can be used to meditate by being "mindful."

Walking meditation

1 *Walk slowly, keeping your body relaxed and your eyes open. Turn your attention to the actions of your body rather than just your breath.*

2 *Be fully conscious of every move you make. Be aware of lifting one foot and putting it in front of the other, as well as your breathing.*

Attention

Meditation doesn't always mean sitting still with your eyes closed. Whatever you are doing, whether it is eating, working on the computer, or washing the automobile, do it with your undivided attention. This practice is called "mindfulness." It sounds much easier than it is. See how long you can hold your attention before your thoughts wander. Mindfulness helps you to be fully present in every moment of the day, without regrets about the past or anxiety for the future. It is a way of bringing meditation into everyday chores.

3 *Feel how your arms are moving. Be conscious of your whole body as a it propels you forward, the blood flowing carrying oxygen to your muscles.*

4 *Concentrate wholly on the present moment, performing every action with your whole attention. You can try this out at intervals during the day.*

meditation in the east

The religions of the East have long used meditation as a means to connect with a deep level of spiritual enlightenment. Many of the techniques used in these traditions are highly practical and effective.

Koans

One of the various ancient meditation schools, Zen Buddhism, uses koans. A koan is a riddle that defies logic.

Probably the most famous koan is, "What is the sound of one hand clapping?" The Zen master chooses a koan for the pupil and tells him or her to go away and

IN DETAIL *The creation of illuminated manuscripts is one form of focussing that Buddhists use as meditation.*

meditate on it with single-minded devotion. This might take the pupil days, weeks, or even years. When the conscious mind finally gives up the impossible task of solving the elusive conundrum, the answer suddenly arises intuitively from the higher consciousness. This is an important lesson in the process of understanding.

ZEN LESSONS *Meditation is a central tool of Zen Buddhists in search of enlightenment and spiritual progress.*

Mandalas

Another ancient method, used particularly in Tibetan Buddhism, is the mandala. This is a symbolic picture incorporating geometrical shapes, especially the square and the circle. Typically, a mandala is divided into four outer sections representing the outer world and a round inner section symbolizing the self. Through contemplating its elaborate imagery, the meditator is led from his or her outer to the inner being, where balance and wholeness are found.

Eight-fold path

A major tenet of eastern meditation is the Buddhist eight-fold path. This embraces right thought, right action, right speech, and right understanding. It is a philosophy of compassion, respecting all beings and harming none. Meditation is viewed as the means of discovering our Buddha nature, which in non-Buddhist circles we might call the true light within.

INTRICATE INSIGHTS *The creation of intricate mandalas is an ancient form of Buddhist meditative practice.*

mantras

A mantra is a word or phrase that is spoken or chanted over and over again, either mentally or aloud. They can be hard to translate, but it is not absolutely necessary to understand exactly what they mean.

Word games

Mantras are words of power. Their effectiveness lies in the vibration of the sound. When they are vibrated correctly the sound strikes a certain frequency, which resonates within the subtle body, stimulating the psychic energy centers and releasing blockages in the energy flow.

The best known mantra is "Om." This is said to be the primal sound, the sound which, going forth at the beginning of time, brought the whole universe into being. Om is a "seed mantra," one from which other mantras are formed. A much-loved mantra is "Om mani padme hum." Approximately translated, this mean "hail to the jewel in the lotus," the jewel being the divine spirit and enlightenment hidden within the lotus of our being.

POWER WORDS *In some Buddhist traditions, enlightenment is thought to be attainable with mantras alone.*

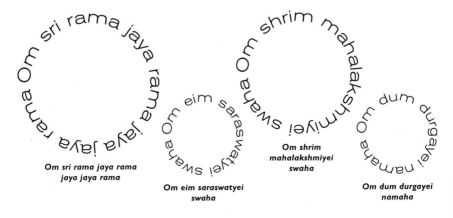

Om sri rama jaya rama
jaya jaya rama

Om eim saraswatyei
swaha

Om shrim
mahalakshmiyei
swaha

Om dum durgayei
namaha

Make your own mantra

In the East, mantras are chosen for a pupil by a teacher. However, you can choose your own. This can be very simple. A single word such as "love" or "harmony" will suffice, or a phrase such as "peace to the world." You can use the name of a spiritual master or even your own name.

There are also plenty of ancient mantras springing from various spiritual traditions. A selection of mantras are provided on page 30. If have a specific religious belief, then try using part of a prayer, hymn, or saying as a mantra.

THE SEED *The most famous mantra is the sound "om." In the Buddhist tradition, this is thought to hold elemental power.*

SOUND FOCUS *As with all meditations, mantras are a way of focusing the mind entirely on a single point.*

31

mantras

The practice of mantras can seem a pretty strange thing to be doing at first. Once you get over your embarrassment, you will find them an immensely rewarding and exciting form of meditation.

om mani padme hum

om mani padme hum om mani

1 *First, take a deep breath into your chest, filling your lungs completely, and relax the throat. Then release your chosen sound on the out breath, half speaking, half chanting on a single note.*

2 *Put your full power and intention behind it. The volume you can produce may surprise you. It is a good idea to ensure that you are in total privacy. Let yourself go and enjoy the sensation.*

Exercise: Working with a Mantra

Decide on the mantra you are going to use. First relax, then repeat the words several times over slowly and purposefully, thinking about what they mean to you. Try to make the sound vibrate. The goal is to focus entirely on the sound and meaning of the word or phrase you are using. Imagine the vibrations of your voice clothing you in the energy of the words.

3 *Let the sound vibrate through your body. Imagine it going out until it fills the universe. You may experience a tingling sensation. This is a sign that you are using the mantra correctly.*

4 *Chant faster until you settle into a rhythm. The words will cease to have meaning; just concentrate on the sound. Go on for five or 10 minutes—then stop—be still—and listen to the silence.*

visualization

Visualization can be either active or passive. In active visualization we focus on an image, then recreate it in the inner vision. In passive meditation we contemplate the images that arise from the inner self.

Picture show

Some people find it easy to see mental pictures. Others believe that it is impossible for them to do so. However, anyone can learn to visualize. Like meditation itself, all it requires is practice and patience. Start with this exercise to get the inner eye opened up:

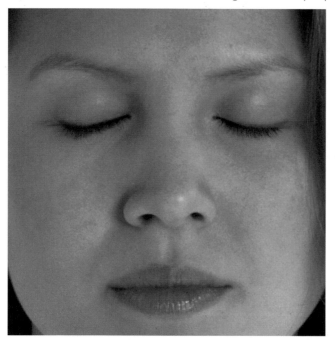

INNER WORLD *Our imagination is far more powerful than many of us think. You can travel anywhere in your mind's eye.*

Exercise: Active visualization

1 *Draw a simple geometrical shape clearly on a large sheet of paper. Gaze at it steadily for a minute or two but don't stare—you are allowed to blink. Then close your eyes and try to see the shape as if it were projected on to a television screen in your forehead. Make it as clear as you can and retain it for as long as possible.*

2 *You can progress from simple images to more complex ones. Choose a picture that appeals to you, or an object, such as a crystal or a flower. As you gaze at it, try to absorb every detail of shape, color, and texture. See how accurately you can reproduce it internally. Then open your eyes and check how much you were able to remember.*

35

pathworking

Pathworking or guided meditation is a form of passive visualization. It uses the imagination as a key for unlocking the unconscious and receiving insights through symbolic images and experiences.

Inner exploration

There are many New Age books, CDs and tapes available that give guided visualizations, or you can create your own. It is best to record the script on tape and play it back when you are meditating. Speak slowly and calmly, allowing plenty of long pauses for the mind to work.

The choice of subjects to use in pathworking is endless, but the scene should be a tranquil one, such as walking in the countryside or strolling along a beach. Try the following example:

YOUR WORLD *Explore your inner world with loving attention and open yourself to the spiritual insights you come across.*

Exercise: Guided visualization

You are walking through a wood... You see the tall trees stretching far above your head... You hear the wind in the branches... You feel the warmth of the sun as it filters through the leaves... To one side is a patch of harebells... Their perfume fills the air... You pick a handful of wild berries... They are deliciously sweet...

As you walk along the path you come to a clearing... In the center of the clearing is a stone circle... Go into the circle... Sense the energy... It is still, yet powerful... In the middle of the circle is a stone altar... Go up to the altar... Touch the stone, feel how cold it is... There is a gold casket on the altar... The casket contains a spiritual gift for you... Open the lid... What do you find?

Now, holding the gift in your hand, turn, and walk out of the stone circle, and down the path through the wood. Feel yourself come firmly back into the body and into your normal state of consciousness. Then open your eyes.

EXPLORE *The only limit to the realms you can explore and the insights you can receive is your own imagination.*

symbols

Symbols often arise spontaneously in meditation. The inner self speaks in pictures rather than in words. If a symbol comes to you, accept it as a message from within. Try to discover what it is saying to you.

Language of objects

Some symbols are universal. They are found in all cultures and religions and arise from the deepest level of mankind's collective unconscious.

For instance, the sun represents the masculine power of the deity, while the moon stands for the eternal cycle of birth and death. The tree is the axis linking this world with the world above. The cross, although now more often associated with Christianity, has been used as a symbol from time immemorial. It has many different uses and associations, including the

point of communication between heaven and earth, and man's dual nature as body and spirit. In the East, the yin yang symbol indicates the union of opposites, light in darkness and darkness in light.

SYMBOL OF BALANCE **This famous Taoist symbol represents yin and yang, the two energies that join to create harmony.**

SACRED FLOWER *The lotus is a central symbol in Buddhism, as Buddha used the flower to teach an important lesson.*

Natural symbols

Animals, birds, and flowers also have significance as symbols. The lion represents strength and the dove gentleness and peace. The lotus flower is a complex symbol. The flower rooted in the muddy waters remind us of our connection with the earth, while the petals opening heavenward symbolize the possibility of spiritual growth and enlightenment.

Beyond all this, however, symbols carry a very personal meaning. If, for instance, in the guided visualization on page 37, your path through the woods has many twists and turns, you might need to consider where your pathway in life is confused. Your "gift" in the casket may indicate a spiritual quality waiting to unfold, such as a pearl for wisdom or a rose for love. Just as in dreams, objects may have special meanings known only to you.

FIND A MEANING *Objects can have thousands of associations. Some, like the rose and the pearl, have universally recognized meanings. They might still have personal resonances completely separate from their common symbolism.*

meditation on the symbol of a lake

If no symbol arises spontaneously for you, try using the image of a lake. Water has many meanings; cleansing, fertility, the unconscious. The lake traditionally represents the soul in which enlightenment is reflected.

Exercise: Meditation on a lake

1 *Relax and calm the mind. Think about a lake. It may help to repeat the word "lake" several times in your mind. Do not try to force the image. Just watch and see what pictures arise in your mind.*

How does your lake appear? Is the water inviting or does it feel dark and threatening? Is it calm or turbulent? Do you feel at peace here? What does this tell you about your inner state?

2 *Think about the significance of water to you. Water may stand for the emotions, so a lake in danger of overflowing might indicate a fear of letting your emotions overwhelm you.*

Dive into the lake and see what lies beneath its surface. What fears lurk here that you need to confront? What potential lies waiting? Keep your mind alert for any insights that arise.

Inner answers

Meditations centering on landscapes, such as this one on the lake, help us to explore our own inner world. We can use a variety of landscapes to explore—mountains, rivers, forests, or even cities. The same guidelines apply as with the lake meditation. Allow the landscape to form itself around you as you explore. In this way your emotions and feelings will be reflected in the features of the landscape. In a forest, for example, do you see a dark, foreboding place or lush, light one?

INTO THE UNKNOWN *Exploring the depths of your inner world can be disquieting at first—but it gets easier.*

opening the third eye

Regular meditation develops the most important psychic center, the brow center, commonly called the "third eye." With practice, we can learn how to use this in our lives.

Power stations

There are seven main energy centers within the body. They are called "chakras," the Sanskrit word for wheel, because they appear clairvoyantly as whirling vortices of light. The chakras are situated in a line along the spine, starting with the root chakra at the base of the spine. Next is the sacral chakra, at the reproductive center, the solar plexus at the navel, the heart, the throat, and the brow. The highest center at the crown of the head is called the thousand-petaled lotus.

As a person begins to evolve spiritually, the chakras start to open and expand, from the lowest upward. The expansion of the solar plexus gives

ENERGY SYSTEM *The chakras were first recognized in the eastern philosophies. Each chakra has specific physical, emotional, and spiritual associations.*

increased sensitivity and intuition. As the heart opens, we are able to give out and receive greater love and compassion. The expansion of the throat center brings creative ability and self-expression, while the crown connects us with the higher dimensions of spirit and with God.

The third eye has always been linked with psychic and occult powers. Pictured as an eye in the middle of the forehead, its development gives the ability to see with the inner vision. This encompasses many things: clairvoyance, seeing spirits, remote viewing or seeing things in distant places, and foreseeing the future. At the highest level, it bestows the gift of spiritual "insight" and spiritual knowledge.

When you begin to see vivid pictures or colors during your meditation, this is a sign that your third eye is developing.

All meditation practices stimulate the development of the third eye, particularly those which involve visualization. The following exercise is particularly helpful because it focuses the attention at the exact point where the third eye is situated.

NEW SIGHT *The development of the third eye through practices such as meditation gives us the gift of insight. We are able to use our intuition to know the truth about convoluted situations.*

opening the third eye

This is a highly practical exercise for helping to develop your third eye. Don't persist in staring at the candle if your eyes begin to tire or feel sensitive. Remember, the focus is not the candle, but your third eye.

Exercise: Candle meditation

1 *Find a candle in a color you like, perhaps white, gold, or purple as these are spiritual colors. The room should be dark. Place the candle on the table about three feet away from you, slightly below eye level. Light it and gaze steadily at the flame. Calm your mind and steady your breathing.*

2 *After a couple of minutes, close your eyes. You will see the after-image of the flame as a small point of white light in your mind's eye, the place between the physical eyes. Keep your attention fixed on this point of light. Do not try to move, control, or change it, just observe.*

Third eye encounters

The third eye has various other names, including "the seat of intuition." By focusing on this area during meditation, we gain a deep and persistent awareness of our intuition and proper judgment. With regular practice, this awareness can reach into our everyday lives. When we make decisions or face difficult situations we will be able to tap into our powers of judgment—instead of relying on external sources for answers to our problems.

3 *The light might appear to move upward. It might change color. Keep it in your inner vision for as long as you can. You may be surprised how long the image remains, sometimes fading and then reappearing again. When it fades completely, open your eyes and look at the candle again.*

4 *Repeat the procedure three times. The last time, try to hold the after-image steady without wavering. When you can no longer see it, keeping your eyes closed, continue to watch the space where it has been. Be aware of any colors or pictures that appear there.*

staying grounded

There is no reason why meditating should make you unable to cope with everyday life. In fact, by bringing yourself into balance and learning to rise above your emotions you will be able to cope better.

Truth finder

Meditation also makes you more intuitive, a valuable asset. It may take the form of inner promptings or just "knowing" when something is going to happen. You might be able to "read" people better and know instinctively when someone is honest and sincere, and when you should be cautious of a person or a situation. These are

positive results of meditation. However, meditating, like everything else, should be done in moderation. If you meditate for excessively long periods of time you may start feeling "spaced out" and detached

DEEP ROOTS *Meditations helps us to see our place in the world, making us feel rooted in our own lives. This brings with it confidence and compassion.*

from reality. Should you find this happening, reduce your meditation time to just a few minutes a day.

Keep a healthy balance in your life by incorporating pastimes of a physical nature, such as exercise, sport, or anything that keeps you in touch with your body. Stay

OUT AND ABOUT *Staying physically fit is an important part of general well-being and promotes mental health.*

GROUNDED *Use this visualization to feel grounded: imagine yourself connected with the earth and all of nature.*

close to nature by gardening or walking in the country. Make time for relaxation and being with friends and family.

New beginnings

Be sure that, at the end of each session, you bring yourself firmly back to your normal state of consciousness. Re-engage with the world, feeling calm and alert.

healing

Our health and well-being is influenced by the subtle energy force, sometimes called chi or prana. This is taken in through the chakras from where it flows out into every part of the body.

Exercise: Balancing chi energy

1 *Sit with your spine erect. Imagine that you have roots going down from your feet and spine into the earth. Take a deep breath and feel the earth energy being drawn up into your feet and legs.*

2 *Take another breath and draw the energy up into the sacral chakra. Then take another breath, and take it up to the solar plexus chakra. Continue in this way through all the chakras.*

Energy cleansing

When the chi energy is in balance we feel well and strong. However, the flow is often blocked through injury, stress, or negative emotions. Meditation rebalances the energy flow and removes blockages. By channeling the energy within us and getting it to flow smoothly, we are carrying out an effective treatment used in many alternative therapies, as well as eastern medicinal traditions—namely the unblocking and balancing of the chakras.

3 *Visualize a golden light above your head. Imagine this light cascading into every cell and atom. Get a sense of these two energy currents, one coming up, the other going down.*

4 *Rest in the energy for a while, allowing it to cleanse and revitalize you. You may feel a tingling sensation as you focus on the energies. Then come back to your normal consciousness.*

setting up a meditation group

However enthusiastic and determined you are, it can be hard to discipline yourself to keep up your practice on a regular basis. Belonging to a meditation group can be a great help.

JOINT PURPOSE *Group meditations can evoke a deep sense of communion and fellowship with the other members.*

Common cause

The group doesn't have to be large—three or four people is enough. But make sure that they are really comfortable with each other and that they share the same general aims and aspirations.

The group should always sit in the same place, at the same time, usually once a week. As with your meditation room, the room you use should be carefully prepared beforehand, simply furnished, and decorated with flowers and suitable pictures. It should be dimly lit and neither too cold nor too hot. Soft, gentle music, incense, and candles help to create a conducive atmosphere.

Sharing energy

A meditation group provides the opportunity for members to experiment with different forms of meditation. Using mantras is particularly rewarding. The joint energy built up by the voices in unison can be thrilling and energizing.

Pathworking is also very suitable. Members can take it in turns to devise and lead the visualizations.

Shared rewards

Sitting in a group gives support. By blending their energy the members are able to reach a deeper state of consciousness than they could achieve individually. The friendship of other people will help maintain your interest and determination, and the members learn from each other by sharing experiences.

ENERGY MERGE *Joint meditation can bring about a powerful feeling of combined energy and purpose.*

the light within

Many people sense that there is a spiritual reality behind the material universe, but they are dissatisfied with orthodox religions. They need to find their own truth, their own connection with the divine.

Remarkable meetings

Making this connection is the most profound meaning of meditation. We all have within us, at the deepest core of our being, an eternal spirit, the over-self or higher self. Symbolically, this is the light within, the jewel in the lotus, or the pearl of great price. It is the point at which we are linked with God, the Source, the Creator, whatever we perceive Him, Her, or It to be. When we are immersed in the material life we have no concept of our true being and reality. But when we go within, the higher self awakens.

SACRED SYMBOLS *In religions all over the world and throughout history, symbols have been used to describe contact with the universal power. This contact is the ultimate goal of meditation.*

Inner chrysalis

This brings about a transformation. Deeper aspects of consciousness begin to unfold. We can start to make sense of life with all its apparent injustices and contradictions. We gain an understanding of what our purpose is and where we fit into the grand scheme of things.

Most of all, we touch the source of all love and light and know that this love and light is within us. The more we meditate, the stronger that light becomes and the more it reaches into every level of our being, helping us to grow.

INNER CHANGE *Contact with the universal power fills us with love and wisdom. The world itself becomes a very different and magical place to us.*

the light within

There are as many experiences of the higher self as there are people who have set out to search for spiritual enlightenment. Try this exercise to as a starting point on your journey of exploration.

Exercise: Connecting with the higher self

This exercise is designed to take you on a journey to the center of your being. Try it when you are in a reflective mood and when you can allow yourself plenty of time to experience and nurture it.

Relax and make yourself very still and quiet. Bring your attention to the body. Be aware of any aches and pains, any uncomfortable sensations. Then mentally put these aside and say to yourself, "I have these sensations but I am not this body."

Next, be aware of your emotions. Are you feeling happy, sad, fearful, anxious? Observe how you are feeling for a few minutes, but from a detached state, then say to yourself, "I have these feelings but I am not these emotions."

HEAD IN THE CLOUDS *Exploration of our spiritual selves brings us to new understanding about the world we live in.*

Then think about your mental processes. What thoughts are uppermost in your mind? Are you thinking about your work, your family, your future? Observe your thoughts as if from a distance and let them go. Say to yourself, "I have these thoughts but I am not this mind."

Now go deeper. Say to yourself, "I am spirit, I am eternal." Focus on this concept until you enter into the point of absolute stillness, the point at which all thought ceases. Then ask yourself calmly and slowly, "Who am I? What is my true self?"

NEW EYES **The discovery and nurture of a spiritual connection within us can transform the way see the world.**

Carry out this exercise as often as you feel inspired to do so. Each time you will receive new and deeper insights into your spiritual nature and develop a stronger connection with your higher self.

This connection with our higher selves often expresses itself in our life with a feeling of not being alone and of inner strength and direction. Accept these gifts and try to remain grateful for them.

the ultimate goal
of meditation

The highest purpose of meditation is to reach a state of enlightenment.
This state is called by many names; nirvana, satori, liberation, god-
realization, cosmic consciousness. It is attainable by all of us.

Mission possible

At this level the meditator dwells in
perpetual bliss, free from all earthly
desires. There is no more sense of
separation between the individual and
God. The spirit becomes at one with all
that is in the the universe. It is released
from the wheel of rebirth, the ceaseless
cycle of earthly incarnations, and has no
need to come to earth again.

In the quest for enlightenment gurus,
saints, and yogis spend many years in
meditation and solitude. Even then, the
search may take many lifetimes. There are
on earth today only a few evolved beings,
such as the much-loved Mother Meera,
who have attained it.

ENLIGHTENED ONE **There are people
who are close to enlightenment. We can
learn from their lives and teachings.**

Obviously, very few people in the western world give up their homes, their families, and their livelihood to pursue this goal. For us, enlightenment remains a very distant prospect indeed, although we may occasionally, in those moments of deep stillness, catch a glimpse of it. But every time we meditate with love in our hearts we move another small step further along the road toward blissful eternity. Yet even those not wishing to take their practice of meditation to this point may still reap benefits that improve their daily lives in countless ways. Meditation will be found to be a practical life skill.

IN THEIR FOOTSTEPS *We can be comforted in our search for the spiritual that many men and women have gone before us: their teachings can guide us.*

NEXT STOP NIRVANA *Buddha is one of the most famous enlightened figures. Many religions center around such pioneers of spiritual exploration, who provide examples for us to follow.*

57

meditation in daily life

Meditation is not an instant cure-all. You need to meditate regularly for several weeks at least before you begin to appreciate its benefits. The effect on your life is so subtle that at first you may not feel any different.

Day to day

In fact, the people around you may notice the change before you do, telling you that you have become less stressed, stronger emotionally, more understanding— generally a nicer person to know.

But the most effective and important transformation is something you will sense in your heart. You will have found a great treasure which is worth more than any of these things. You will have discovered your spirit—your deepest being.

This inner knowing is a great source of strength. It gives you the self-esteem to be true to yourself in the way you live your life. You find the courage to express yourself and speak your own truth not with negative arrogance, but with firmness, conviction, compassion, and understanding.

DAILY ROUTINE *If we fit meditation into our daily routine, it will start to affect the way we work on a day-to-day basis.*

Far from being a selfish activity, as is sometimes thought, meditation is perhaps the most valuable service you can perform for others. Every person who meditates lights a candle to help others find their way; and all these little candles, shone by meditators everywhere, may help to bring much-needed healing to the world.

ENDLESS SEARCH *Meditation does not have an point at which we stop and say "Done that." Regular practice takes us ever further into the spiritual realm, we need only be open to new revelations.*

glossary

Aura Electromagnetic energy field around the human body

Chakra Energy center within the human body

Chi In Eastern tradition, the vital life force energy

Cosmic consciousness Condition of being at one with God

Icon Religious picture used for devotional purposes

Koan An insoluble mental puzzle, used in Zen meditation

Mandala Religious picture incorporating geometrical designs, symbolizing wholeness

Mantra Repeated word or phrase that brings about an altered state of consciousness

Meditation Art of centering the mind in order to connect with the inner self

Mindfulness Meditation technique of focusing wholly on the present moment

Nirvana In Buddhist tradition, state of enlightened bliss

Pathworking Guided visualization on images arising from the unconscious

Satori State of experience of enlightenment

Third eye Energy center in the brow connected with inner vision

Visualization Art of creating images in the inner vision

Yang In Chinese thought, a principle seen as masculine, light, warm, and active

Yin In Chinese thought, a principle seen as feminine, dark, cold, and passive

index

acknowledgments

Thanks to the following for their help with producing this book:
The Stone Corner, 42a High Street, Hastings, Sussex, England TN34 3ER
Mysteries Ltd., 9–11 Monmouth Street, Covent Garden, London, England, WC2H 9DA
The Pier, 200 Tottenham Court Road, London, England, W1P 0AD
Picture Credits: The Hutchinson Library: 28bl, 28tr, 29b, 31r, 56